I THINK YOU SHOULD TALK TO SOMEONE

Mercutio The Bard

Copyright © 2021 Mercutio The Bard

All rights reserved

The right of Mercutio The Bard to be identified as the author of this work has been asserted by him in accordance with the Copyright, Designs and Patents Act 1988.

Paperback ISBN: 9798783116056
Hardback ISBN: 9798783225468

This book is dedicated to anyone who ever needed to talk about their feelings, but felt as though they couldn't.

I NEVER THOUGHT I'D BE AROUND TO WRITE THIS

They say that there is no longer a stigma about mental health.

I disagree, I have found that whilst more people nowadays are championing that it's OK to talk about mental health,
in practice, most people don't really want to listen.

'I THINK YOU SHOULD TALK TO SOMEONE" is a phrase that I'm sure many readers will have heard. I know I have!

Whilst people do often mean well, this is a phrase that tends to shut down the conversation.

"I thought I was talking to someone?" I always think when I hear this.
"Oh, you mean a professional.... Thanks for listening"

It takes a huge amount of courage to talk. If someone who is struggling confides in you - Please be brave enough to listen to them.

This book is dedicated to anyone who has ever needed to talk about their feelings, but felt as though they couldn't.

I hope that you will find some comfort in the words I have written, that they might show you some solidarity and bring some reassurance that you are not alone.

I hope also that these poems will help those who are close to people who are struggling, to better understand what they are experiencing.

No two struggles are the same, my words are based on my own experiences and on my own journey navigating the darkness of despair. I understand that all journeys are unique and I respect all who bravely venture through that dark.

I just want you to know that you are not alone and that despite how hopeless it may seem, with the right approach, it does get better.

Take each moment as it comes and remember that you are not your thoughts - You are the one that observes them.

With love and respect,

Mercutio The Bard

WHAT TO EXPECT

I must warn you upfront, that this book tackles some disturbing issues that some readers may find triggering.

The poetry in this book reflects the depths of mental struggles in the most poignant way that I can articulate and as such things get a little dark at times.

Stick with it.

Much like my own journey out of the darkness, these poems will take you through a journey from despair to hope, from darkness to light, from resistance to acceptance and from disparagement to gratitude.

These poems are intended to be read aloud, even if you whisper them so quietly that the sound barely escapes your lips, please approach them in this manner.

They are purposefully concise and should be read and re-read as many times as are necessary.

Take a pen and scribble down your thoughts. Make your own notes in the spaces available on the pages and if you feel that they articulate your own struggles in a way that you have found difficult to explain, then please share them with those who you hold close. In hope that it may bring them some understanding of how you feel.

If you feel the need to talk to someone about your feelings then please have the courage to do so.

This world can be a beautiful place if you let it, but it's hard to see that beauty when you are lost in the dark.

I wish you strength, courage and enlightenment on your journey.

And most of all,

I wish you peace.

LET'S TALK ABOUT IT

This one's for the kid in the class that won't smile

This one's for the kid in the class that won't laugh

This one's for the kid in the class that needs help

This one's for the kid in the class that won't ask

This one's for the mother that's at her wits end

This one's for the dad who has no time to lend

This one's for the grieving - It isn't your fault

This one's for anyone who needs to talk

This one's for the listeners, the heroes, the friends

This one's for the desperate - There's light at the end

This one's for the survivors - I salute you

This one's from me - In hope it helps you

WHERE ANGELS FELL

Where once saints made gods of men

Remember also just as well

That in amongst the ranks of them

Angels fell where Demons dwell

BLACK DOG

I have a black dog that follows me around

It hides in every smile

Grits it's teeth through every frown

I have a black dog that won't leave me alone

It barks so I ignore the calls

My friends make to my phone

I have a black dog that watches as I weep

It curls up there beside me

But doesn't ease my grief

I have a black dog that interrupts my sleep

With howls of insecurity

And anxious biting teeth

I have a black dog that no one else can see

It's probably just as well

Or else they'd all think I'm crazy

I have a black dog that scratches at my door

I'm told I shouldn't feed it

But it keeps demanding more

I have a black dog that scares my dreams away

It tears into my every hope

With fangs, like lifeless prey

I have a black dog that brings an air of gloom

It covers every ray of light

And darkens every room

I have a black dog that always has me stressing

I have a black dog

A dog I call "Depression"

DEPRESSION

Smothering

A feeling like drowning

In air

Whilst everyone else about you floats by gracefully

Sinking

In a sea of silent suffering

Staring out of misted windows at nothing

For hours

Solemn strained smiles decorate brave faces

Masking the misery unseen

At least it seems

But teary eyes tell no lies

Acting as though everything is fine

Because on paper at least it appears to be

And yet despite these serene times

You feel instead only misery

When everything is going great

And yet you still can't bear to face

The light of day as though the sun's rays

Burn your fragile soul

Proceeding to pretend

All's well to family and friends

Whilst battling demons deep within

The great charade continues

The dread of knowing

That something is deeplywrong

Whilst in the hazy background

The melancholy music of your sad and sombre song

Plays on

Broken, shaky, dead inside

Yet when somebody asks

"How are you?"

Every single time

You reply

"I'm Fine"

SOMETHING'S WRONG

Something's really wrong inside my mind

Something's disconnected I can feel it all the time

Ask me how I feel I'll say I'm fine

I've mastered this mask I wear

I wear it all the time

Something's really wrong inside my mind

Something unexpected

I've expected for some time

Ask me how I feel I'll say I'm fine

I've mastered telling twisted truths

I'm lying all the time

SUFFOCATING

I properly cannot breathe

I'm suffocating

Straining to make head or tail of when or where I'm supposed to be

Lost in mediocracy

Wondering what possibly

Could have been - Would have been

How everything should have been

Distinctly differently

Save me - Or Better yet - Pray for me - To save myself

To jump down from that dusty shelf

And breathe some life into myself

I'm down on luck and low on wealth

And struggling with mental health

I want to fix things by myself

But truthfully I need some help

I need a friend - I need someone

Who understands where I've come from

Who's travelled down the path I'm on

Who knows the turns - left, right or wrong

I wanna shout - I wanna sing

I wanna achieve everything

I've always dreamed of achieving

But fear can stop you believing

I feel like soon I'll be leaving

To wander a familiar road

And finish off a journey that I started a long time ago

And I want to go - I want to leave

I want to be all I can be - I desperately want to believe

But right now I just need to breathe

I wish the world would ease it's grip

I'm suffocating coz of it

CARRY ON

Stuck somewhere between ugly and vanity

Stranded between genius and insanity

Broken - Wishing someone would carry me

Choking or to put it in my Granny's tongue

"I canne breathe"

Leave me here to die - Just carry on

It's hard to be a prince without a king to guide you

It's hard to live

When everything around you seems so long

It's hard to carry on

Oh, what a carry on

BE STRONG

I know it's tough but you are strong enough

I know it hurts but that is love my love

I know it's hard but you've waited long enough

I know you're tired but darling don't give up

I know it's dire and it's eating you alive

Beating you up inside - Be kind - To yourself

I know it's tough and you feel like giving up

But keep on keeping on - I believe in you

I know it's long and you're barely holding on

But you've got this you're so strong

It's not long now

I know your smile hides - The bitterness inside

The millions of times you've cried - Alone

Please just hold on - Darling - Be strong

IT'S NOT YOUR TIME

I know it's not your time

But darling close your eyes

And hold my hand so tight

It's gonna be alright

I know it's not your time

But darling close your eyes

You put up such a fight

Sleep tight

It's gonna be alright

MISSING YOU

Close the curtain

I never noticed you were hurting

I've had no time to cry for you

I've been too busy working

Now I'm certain

These raindrops on the window

Stain my memories of us

Stuck - I'm lost in limbo

And I'm searching

For a little piece of you

But I can't find it anywhere

I don't know what to do

I know you're out there

Coz I can still feel you

And no amount of counselling

Can change my point of view

I miss you

And it's breaking me inside

Now I can't carry on no more

I need to run and hide

And try to find you - To find a reason why

You made that brash decision

And left me here behind

And I know that there's no turning

Back the hands of time

But I won't forgive myself unless I try

I'm waiting

Please show me a sign

The days, the weeks, the months, the years

The memories all disappear

They're fading - So I try to cling to you

Coz all that I have left is that rough sketch that you once drew

In the studio - Back when I still had you

And everything was doom and gloom

But you carried me through

Was it too much?

Was my pain affecting you?

I never meant to hurt you - I just didn't deserve you

Now It's too late

I'm running out of time

I'm too tired to carry on - Pretending that I'm fine

Im not - I'm dying

And lying when I'm smiling

Because inside I'm crying - Crying out for you

The tears keep falling

These sad stains on my cheeks

Keep me from recalling

The times when I knew peace

And I keep calling

But you're number's disconnected

And I know this but it's hopeless

I'm so bitterly affected

I miss you

And it's breaking me inside

Now I can't carry on no more

I need to run and hide

And try to find you

To find a reason why

You made that brash decision

And left me here behind

And I know that there's no turning

Back the hands of time

But I won't forgive myself unless I try

BREAKING

Feel like I'm about to break down

Feel like I'm about to take flight

Feel like I'm about to get drowned

Feel like I'm not destined for life

Feel like I'm not meant for success

Feels like I'm awake every night

Feeling like I'm losing my mind - I feel like

Feel like taking my life

Feel like I'm breaking inside

Feel like I'm right on the edge

Feel like I'm living a lie

Feel like I'm losing my head

Feel like I'm aching inside

Feel like I'm out on a ledge

Feel like I'm ready to die - This feels like

Feels like

This is the end

I don't wanna live no more - Like this

I don't wanna see another sunset on this lonely-lonely island

I'm dying inside - Although I try to hide

Behind a smile - You can see it in my eyes

I'm so tired - Of all of this violence

Sleepless city nights - Alive with passing sirens

Another story ended - Another night pretending

That everything's OK - But it ain't

I feel like I'm breaking down

CHRISTMAS JUMPER

What if I threw myself in front of this train?

Would I feel pain?

Would it be worse than the pain that I'm feeling?

Would it be worse than what's happening in my brain?

Would it be worse than waiting?

Would it be worse than standing here in the rain?

Would it be worse than the fate that I'm already facing?

Would it put an end to this game?

Would these Christmas shoppers think that it's a shame?

Or just be mad their journey is delayed?

HOW TO STAY ALIVE

I recall the last time that I saw you smile

It was winter time and you were playing in the snow

I'd forgotten how your laughter used to lift the mood

And even in my darkest hours

How your vibrance glowed

I recall the happiness once in your eyes

I remember how it softly dulled

I wish I could take you back to better times

But I fear you wouldn't want to go

And I knew that something sad was happening

I could see the trauma in your eyes

I'd have sat up with you for a thousand nights

If only I could try

To show you how to stay alive

BITTER

I made my bed this morning - Now it's a total mess

I left the kitchen tidy - Now there's no glasses left

I drink straight from the bottle - I'm drinking to forget

I jump into my motor - And drive to Inverness

Bitter taste of bitter pills - I'm drinking to forget

Bitter taste of bitter pills - I've not got long left

Bitter at the bitterness - Bitter at this mess

Bitter taste O' bitter fate - Lay me down to rest

The lights are bright they're blinding - I'm veering to the left

Trying to reach the bottle - That fell down by the armrest

The road signs fuzzy blurry - I'ts spinning out my head

I missed my turning now I'm burning in a bloody wreck

Bitter taste of bitter pills - I'm drinking to forget

Bitter taste of bitter pills - I've not got long left

Bitter at the bitterness - Bitter at this mess

Bitter taste O' bitter fate - Lay me down to rest

I lost my life this evening - I'm dreaming from the dead

I lost control and now my friends are mourning me instead

I left my music playing out from speakers by my bed

Now I'm no longer tired - I finally got to rest

Bitter taste of bitter pills - There's no more to forget

Bitter taste of bitter pills - I knew I'd not long left

Bitter at the bitterness - Not bitter with regret

Bitter taste O' bitter fate - Lay me down to rest

SNOW FALL AT SEA

Alone and afraid

His passing left no trace

Like snow fall at sea

The waves washed his legacy

NIGHT TERRORS

Another sleepless night

Sat perched precariously on the edge of the bed

Sweating profusely

Head filled with dread

Heart pierced with the sharp pangs of anguish

The heavy weight of worry bearing down

Upon my weakening frame

These once proud shoulders now sloping solemnly

Down towards the ground

All but every last sign of strength

Sapped from their sorry shape

love replaced by hate

Hope drowned in fear

Loathing, foreboding

Bitterness and dark

The cold night's shadow

Creeps in through the crack in the curtain

And envelopes me in shame

I feel it pulsing through my very being

Itching in my fingertips

Coasting through my veins

Physical pain

Actual real discomfort

Boring through my aching bones

And crippling me in shaky silence

Too many questions

So many variables

Infinite unknowns and endless uncertainty

It's hurting me

This will be the death of me most certainly

Perhaps I'll see things clearer in the light of day

But tomorrow seems like it's an eternity away

I find myself believing I should pray

But can't remember how to speak to deities that way

So still I sit and wait

My thoughts race

My hands shake

I'm not sure I will make it through this test

This stress is haunting every thought

My mind's a bloody mess

Dry throat

Tight chest

Anxiety manifest

ANXIETY

Tick

Fingers fidget

Knees knock

Feet shuffle

Pulse races

Time ticks too fast

As unfulfilled moments pass

This fragile day will never last

Until tomorrow

Tick, tock

Hurry

Quickly, start that which you intend to finish
Soon

Before it becomes too late.

Tick, tock, tick

Late

Late for what?

For nothing

Waiting, impatiently

Anticipating absolutely nothing

Mind concerned with absolutely everything

Consumed by an all-encompassing passing of time

That most precious commodity

Tick, tock, tick, tock

I feel its golden sands slip through my aging fingertips

And I regret each fleeting moment

That I spent deliberating

Tick, tock, tick

Heart aching pangs of should a, would a

Could a been a something

Could a been an anything

An everything

A somebody

Instead I dread the passing of another sun

Beyond that bleak horizon

That my muddled mind has come to know familiar

Another wasted day gone by

Another great intention slayed

By time's cruel passing

Tick, tock

Cold sweats

Clammy palms

Dead arms and tired legs

The sordid realisation that Monday once again has come

And I must still embark upon this beaten path of drudgery

Oh,

What torment I have set before me

Oh,

What dreams I left lost aloft clouded memories

Tick

Fingers fidget

Knees knock

Feet shuffle

Pulse races

Late again

Too busy doing nothing

FALSE SMILES

False smiles are often so alluring

Heed not their deciet

Look to the eyes instead

For there hides the truth

TEARS UNSEEN

The blind lead wearily

Along treacherous roads

Cautiously following the murmurs of the mute

Their silent statements fall upon deaf ears

Whilst closed eyes stream tears unseen

HIS BIGGEST REGRET

Years of hard graft and sweat

His weathered hands marked his efforts

To provide for them

His absence

To them

Marked his neglect

Those precious moments that he missed

His biggest regret

LITTLE ONE

Little one

Don't grow up so quick

One day soon the shoe will fit

Until then.....

Keep your head held high

And never stop believing

ARMOURED SMILE

She wore her smile bravely

Like a shining suit of armour

Beneath which she flinched

At every blow they'd throw at her

KIND RAGE

In defiance of his burning rage

Her gentle kindness

Disarmed him

SELF-DEPRECIATION

She held onto her regret as though

It was the only thing that made her human

The knowledge that she had done so wrong

To so many

Somehow brought some form of respite

To her inner pain

But as others looked upon her

All they saw

Was the kindness which she had shown them

Yet she still could not forget

Her own vile version of the past

She felt as though her truth was an imposter

A twisted lie

TELL ME

Tell me something I don't know about you

See the truth that lies inside of me

There is something beautiful about you

A glimmer in your eyes that I can see

TIGER STRIPES

The tiger stripes sit softly on her arm

Their crimson colour covering her history of harm

Scars etched deep within her flesh she feels regret

She can't forget her daft attempts to find her inner calm just yet

It's best the past is left behind like torn and tattered garms

A fortune hard to read amongst the wet of sweaty palms

The blade itself incites her to inflict another harm

So deep the cut that when she bleeds she sings the devil's psalm

And somewhere deep beneath the surface something scary hides

And sometimes when she's all alone she feels it come alive

And sometimes when she's all alone she cannot help but cry

Those tiger stripes remind her how she very nearly died

Sometimes she'd rather hide

Than have to face the bright

City streets that pass her by with all their blinding lights

These ever lonely nights merge into ever hopeless days

She doen't know what's worse to be asleep or be awake

She doesn't know her worth - She gave it all away

She doesn't recognise the hurt - She's numb now to it's pain

And there are many secrets she will carry to her grave

But those tiger stripes do little good to hide from where she came

The bitterness and shame that clouds her own demise

Her smile's so bright but there is such a sadness in her eyes

And in the moment that she feels to quit

Once more she tries

Her best to stay alive

The tiger must survive

IT'S HARD TO TELL YOU

Every single time

I try to find the words

To tell you how I feel

My heart breaks a little

MISSING YOU

My days are long without you

My nights are cold and lonely

My soul is quiet without you

My heart weeps softly, slowly

SNOW QUEEN

Glistening in the early morning moonlight

Frost shines bright off the leaves like diamonds

Crystals softly fade as bitter ice melts

Beneath the warm touch of the rising sun

But right now in this moment

Perfect - frozen

These diamonds aren't forever

But for now my dear

They are for you

POKER FACE

He saw her heart

And raised her a diamond

He was all in

She folded and left him

FAST LOVE

Her love came fast

Like the darkness at dusk

And filled my spirit with the essence of her presence

But she departed in an instant

A thunder and a flash

Like the morning breaks the night before

Discarding my passion with reckless abandon

And leaving my lonely sky void of stars

BLOOD MONEY

It's crazy how these kids behave for money

It's their vice

The paper their placebo

This greed disease is rife

Some droplet of decorum would be nice

Instead they honour profit

With their selfish sacrifice

Consider those around you would be my advice

An apology or even acknowledgement would suffice

Fool me once, twice, deny me thrice

Even Judas in his dying moments wept for Christ

MUDDLED

Muddled in a muddy puddle

Pondering these murderous schemes

Most malicious are these mutineers

So it would seem

THE WORLD IS ON FIRE

The world is burning whilst the man plays golf

He can barely see the T

Through the thickening smoke

The hills are alive with an amber glow

As he watches the inferno from the 18th hole

BUSY ROADS

Take a moment

Pause

Look around you

Take it in

All that you have

Appreciate

Witness

Know

Trees don't grow on busy roads

COFFEE

Oh sweet-bitter coffee

How art thou so persuasive?

As to drag me from such heavy slumber

And ready me for the day

BOOKS

I love the smell of old books

And the sweet escape they bring

As rain drums on my window

on lazy afternoons

IN A WORD

What is a story without any words?

What is an action without any verbs?

What is a person without any nouns?

What is a saying without any sound?

What am I - In a word?

I am here - And I am grateful

MISSED MOMENTS

Take me back

To a time without schedule

To a place without destination

A memory

I forgot

Was once a moment

That I missed

DO TODAY

Do today

That which you may

Hope to do tomorrow

Time will not wait

NOTHING LEFT

Nothing left to do

Nothing left to prove

You'll finally find freedom when you've

Nothing left to lose

KEEP ON KEEPING ON

Take a second stop and look around you

Wonder at how far along you've come

Forget all the fuckeries that found you along the way

They made you wiser

Made you braver

Made you strong

You've journeyed so far from where you started

Even though the path sometimes feels long

If you don't know where you're headed

How can you possibly go wrong?

Just keep on keeping on

You can feel the child inside you

As though they're stood beside you

Tugging at your coat tails

Trying to remind you

Always to be mindful

Trying to inspire you

To live inside the moment

Don't let your vision blind you

Don't let your demons haunt you

Your past no longer binds you

Coz memory's a liar

There's a reason it's behind you

And the future can't be certain

So don't get so worried

Take time whilst you're here right now

This moment can't be hurried

Take a second stop and look around you

Wonder at how far along you've come

Forget all the fuckeries that found you along the way

They made you wiser

Made you braver

Made you strong

You've journeyed so far from where you started

Even though the path sometimes feels long

If you don't know where you're headed

How can you possibly go wrong?

Just keep on keeping on

RAIN DANCE

And just as the sunny season

Gives way to rain

So too will come for you

A time of change

Let the downpour wash away

Your pain

Dance amongst the puddles

Learn to laugh again

REMEMBER THIS

Remember this

This feeling that you're feeling

This pain inside your being

Your dreams can manifest

Remember this

This feeling that you're feeling

Never stop believing

It won't always be like this

Remember this

MAY YOU FIND YOUR PEACE

Thank you for taking the time to read this collection of poetry. I am grateful to be able to share these words with you and I hope that you have gained something valuable from them.

I wish you peace on your journey.

With love and respect,

Mercutio The Bard

A LIGHT TO GUIDE YOU

The journey out of the darkness is an arduous one and one to which you must find your own unique path.

Here are some simple things that I practice daily which have helped me on my own journey.

I am sharing them with you in the hope that they may help you too.

1) When I wake up in the morning, typically to the sound of my alarm, I instinctively think "Oh for f*ck sake". When this happens, I consciously check myself and say to myself "You don't HAVE to get up - you GET to get up". I find that this simple exercise helps to start the day in a more positive way.
Each day is a new opportunity to find peace. Be grateful that you get to try again. You will get there in the end.

2) Be present in the moment. This is not always possible as at times you will need to either remember past events or plan for future ones, however by consciously focussing on the present as much as possible you will find much comfort and peace.
Most people tend to spend most of their time either thinking about the past (which can stimulate depression) or thinking about the future (which can stimulate anxiety). Occassionally people will have a moment of clarity, perhaps during a holiday in a

moment of relaxation or quite the opposite, during a moment of intense danger or excitement, where they will suddenly become very aware of the present moment.

These glimpses of clarity tend to bring a deep sense of calm, even in the most frightening situations.

These moments of mindfulness are the natural state intended for a person and the more time that you can spend in the present moment, the more you will benefit your wellbeing.

The truth is that there is only the present moment. The past no longer exists and the future is yet to be decided.

So live in the the moment, for that is all there really is.

3) Listen to music. Listen to different types of music and feel how your mind and body responds. Create different playlists for different moods and use them to help you to take more control over your feelings.

4) Appreciate the little things in life. Spend more time in nature. Walk more slowly, consciously taking in what you see and hear around you. There really is so much beauty in the world if you take time to really witness it.

5) Eat well. I'm not saying that you need to go full vegan plant based diet. But there is a definite connection between what you put into your body and how it affects your mood.

6) Sleep well. Try to get a decent amount of sleep. Tiredness can have a really negative effect on your ability to cope with stress. There are lots of really good sleep playlists available to help with deep sleep and some great herbal teas to take before bed.

7) Move well. Try to exercise. Not so much for how it will make you

look, but more for how it will make you feel. find activities that you enjoy doing and make time to do them regularly.

8) Meditate. Take time each day to be still and focus on your breathing. Thoughts will come and go, do not fight them, simply acknowledge them and let them pass. Daily meditation will help massively to reduce stress levels.

9) Water. The life force of the planet. Drink plenty of water. I talk to my water before I gulp it down. Think of it what you will, but I'm convinced that it has a healing effect. I whisper positive affirmations to my water before I drink it.

Also, take time regularly to relax in the bath or shower. Water can be very calming if you visualise it washing away your negative thoughts and feelings.

10) Don't be too hard on yourself. The pendulum swings perpetually. There will be good days and there will be bad days. Try to take each day in your stride. Deal with each and every moment as it comes and give yourself permission to ride the waves. Remember, you are not your thoughts, you are the one who observes them. Allow negative and positive thoughts to flow freely and don't attach too much energy to them. A wise guru once told me that you should never get too excited and never get too upset. To maintain balance within the swing of the pendulum is to find your peace.

I hope that some of these practices may help you.

Everyone's journey is unique, so do what works best for you.

May you find your peace.

With love and respect,

Mercutio The Bard

ABOUT THE AUTHOR

Mercutio The Bard

A collection of poems from acclaimed word-smith:

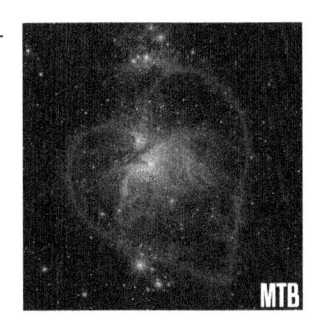

MERCUTIO THE BARD

I THINK YOU SHOULD TALK TO SOMEONE explores the unseen interior of a struggling mind through concise and thought provoking poetry.

Honest, vulnerable and poetically profound, this collection of poems offers an intimate insight into the author's perspective on life.

Profoundly poignant, punchy poetry with a deeper meaning, this book is dedicated to anyone who has ever needed to talk about their feelings, but felt as though they couldn't.

BOOKS BY THIS AUTHOR

Musings & Mutterings Of A Madman

Modern poetry for a mad world.

A collection of poems from acclaimed wordsmith:

MERCUTIO THE BARD

Musings & Mutterings Of A Madman tackles the everyday struggles of a creative mind trying to navigate this crazy world.

Honest, vulnerable and poetically profound, this collection of poetry and prose offers an intimate insight into the author's perspective on life. With gripping storytelling and rhythmic writing, this book is a must for anyone who struggles with the madness of modern life.

Limited Edition Special Photo Book edition available signed by the author on request.

Email: mercutio.the.bard@gmail.com

An Anthology Of Bars

Life in lyrics.

A collection of poems from acclaimed wordsmith:
MERCUTIO THE BARD

AN ANTHOLOGY OF BARS showcases the depth of lyricism attainable through the medium of rap.

Funny, fearless and fervently flawless, this collection of lyrics read like an anthology of poetry.
With technical rhyme schemes and eloquently articulated flow patterns, the author holds nothing back in exhibiting the incredible word play which has earned him respect amongst some of the UK's top rapper and producers.
Known as a lyrical heavyweight on the underground Hip Hop circuit, Mercutio The Bard breaks down some of his most potent bars in this epic anthology.

A must read for fans of rap music and lyricism and for all students of poetry.